INDEX

APPENDICES

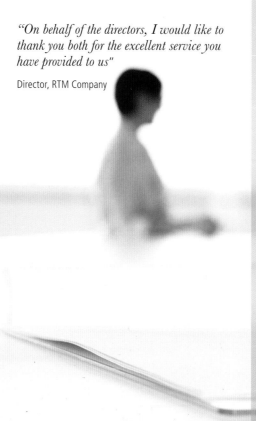

"Thank you for your helpful guidance relating to the appointment of new directors….Your guidance on the eligibility of potential directors is particularly helpful as I need to ensure that any owner wanting election is not doing so in order to avoid proceedings against him/her for non-payment of management charges"

RMC Company Director

"I thank you in advance and for all the support and help you have given me while being a Director of …. Management Company Limited."

"First of all let me thank you for your flawless work you have done in the past for me. I had trouble free experience and I hope it will continue in the future."

Director of two RTM Companies

"Thank you again for the outstanding work you have done"

Director, RTM Company

"On behalf of the directors, I would like to thank you both for the excellent service you have provided to us"

Director, RTM Company

INTRODUCTION

A flat is not like a house. You cannot make decisions about maintenance and cleaning on your own. The protection of the quality and value of your asset is in the hands of a group of people you hardly know and with whom you probably did not specifically choose to live.

You may well have a Managing Agent. We joke that people hate their Managing Agent because we take more of your money than you would like and spend more of it than you would want on your private home without your permission.

The Directors of your Residents' Management ("RMC") or Right to Manage ("RTM") Company are in virtually all cases unpaid volunteers. Without them, your asset and environment could degenerate into a slum. They are the unsung heroes of the residential property market. They take risks, put up with aggravation they do not need and spend their private time and considerable effort for your benefit.

You may have received this booklet because somebody thinks you would be a great addition to the pool of expertise that is the Board of your RMC or RTM. If so, we do hope you will seriously consider doing a term of office to help the community in your building.

We have written this to help potential RMC and RTM Directors understand what is involved in running a building as a Company Director. It may also be a useful refresher for existing Directors, but our hope is that it will inspire and encourage more people to get involved.

Jim Thornton BSc(Hons) MA CEng MICE MCIOB MARLA MIRPM is a Chartered Civil Engineer and Builder and is Managing Director of Hurford Salvi Carr Property Management Ltd. He is a Director of 21 companies including a PLC and a South African subsidiary and is Company Secretary of 96 companies. He has been a Managing Director since the age of 29 and is a Trustee of several Charitable Trusts.

Janette Leaf MA read English at Cambridge and since 2000 has run the Company Secretariat and Right to Manage services at Hurford Salvi Carr Property Management Ltd during which time she has looked after more than 100 RMC and 60 RTM Companies.

The first thing you must do is get hold of a copy of the **Memorandum & Articles of Association of the Company**.

We will assume this is a Residents' Management Company, which we will call **Magnificent Mansions Management Ltd**, or '**MMM**' for short.

To help you analyse it, Appendix I has an analysis of the Statutory Articles of Association of a Right to Manage Company and we have provided a blank column where you can tick where it agrees if your own building has a Residents' Management Company.

The Company is a separate legal entity from its directors, shareholders and employees. *The best interests of the Company are not always the same as the best interests of the shareholders.*

What are Memorandum and Articles (Mem & Arts) ?

The Articles of Association define the rules governing how the Company is to be run, including what the directors' powers and responsibilities are.

The Articles also set out how decisions are to be taken: for example, the procedures for calling a board meeting and how many directors are needed to vote on a proposal.

You must act within the powers granted in the Articles of Association.

You can only change the Company's objects by getting shareholder agreement.

If the Directors act outside the Company's objects, the Company may be entitled to take legal action against them.

Companies set up since 1 October 2009 are not restricted in their objectives ('objects') unless their Articles of Association say otherwise.

Companies set up prior to 1 October 2009 listed their objects in the Memorandum of Association. These are now deemed to be part of the Articles unless a resolution to remove them has been passed.

AM I ELIGIBLE TO BE A DIRECTOR OF MMM?

You cannot be a Director if:

- You are under 16
- You are an undischarged bankrupt
- You have been disqualified (for misbehaving as a Director previously)
- You are the auditor
- or if the Mem & Arts have a restriction with which you don't comply, such as 'only flat owners can be Directors'. Being a resident in the building probably isn't enough.

SECOND QUESTION: WHAT RESPONSIBILITIES WOULD I HAVE AS A DIRECTOR OF MMM?

The Companies Act 2006 sets out the **Statutory Duties** owed by the Directors to MMM in Part 10 (SS.170-181). These are that you have a duty:

- to act within powers (as set out in the Mem & Arts)
- to promote the success of the company
- to exercise independent judgement
- to exercise reasonable care, skill and diligence
- to avoid conflicts of interest
- not to accept benefits from third parties
- to declare an interest in any proposed transaction or agreement

This all sounds a bit theoretical, so what does it mean in practice? **The Institute of Directors** Fact Sheet summarises it a bit more succinctly:

The Board of Directors of a company is primarily responsible for:

- Determining the company's strategic objectives and policies;
- Monitoring progress towards achieving the objectives and policies;
- Appointing senior management;
- Accounting for the company's activities to relevant parties.

In other words, for MMM you are primarily responsible for:

- Setting a Service Charge Budget for the year ahead including a Reserve Fund collection in accordance with the lease provision
- Monitoring expenditure and compliance with the lease during the year
- Appointing a Managing Agent and ensuring they perform the services as set out in the Management Agreement
- Circulating Certified or Audited Service Charge Accounts within six months of the year end and ensuring proper returns are sent to Companies House and HMRC

Success?

What does 'promote the success of the company' mean?

The Act says it means the Director must 'have regard to':

- The likely consequences of any decision in the long term
- The interests of the company's employees
- The need to foster the company's business relationships with suppliers, customers and others
- The impact of the company's operations on the community and the environment
- The desirability of the company maintaining a reputation for high standards of business conduct; and
- The need to act fairly as between members of the company

What is a Shadow Director?

Even if you have never been appointed a Director, you could be classed as a shadow director (if the other directors are 'accustomed to act' under your instructions) or as a 'de facto' director if you act as if you were one – for example, if you resign but continue giving instructions.

As a shadow director or de facto director you carry many of the legal responsibilities and are subject to many of the penalties, of other directors.

THIRD QUESTION:
WHAT LIABILITIES WOULD I HAVE AS A DIRECTOR OF MMM?

Do not be scared off by what follows: leaseholders throughout the country owe an enormous debt of gratitude to the volunteer Directors whose unpaid hard work protects the values of the flats in their building. If the downside was so great, nobody would do the job.

Providing you act honestly and thoughtfully you have nothing to fear and MMM ought definitely to have Directors' & Officers' Insurance (does it? Do check).

Do also check that your Managing Agents or any other advisers have suitable Professional Indemnity cover and that there is a procedure in place to check the insurances of all contractors.

Directors & Officers Insurance

D&O insurance covers past, present and future directors in respect of breaches of duty by directors and officers in managing and directing their company's affairs. Individual's can be held personally liable for their actions/decisions and may not be able to afford the costs of defending legal actions against them.

Cover includes:

- Claims and circumstances first made against the insured and notified to insurers during the policy period
- events that may have occurred prior to the inception of the policy
- Legal Representatives clause providing protection in the event of death, incompetence, incapacity or bankruptcy of insured persons;
- Defence Costs for insured persons in fraud and dishonesty actions or in defending an action for illegal remuneration, until there is a final judgement
- Main Exclusions: fines and penalties

Claims examples from Residents Associations (kindly provided by Locktons)

- A resident requested that trees near the individuals flat were pollarded. Although the trees were subject to regular maintenance, squirrels entered the occupier's roof void from overhanging branches causing damage to the property. The occupier alleged that this was as a result of negligence by the committee. Assistance was provided in resolving the dispute
- There was an alleged breach of the Data Protection Act. Insurers provided support and legal assistance in ensuring that the commissioner was satisfied that no breach occurred. Cost were in the order of £15k
- Defending a civil action against the directors of the RA for alleged sale of common parts below value. Defence costs in region of £30k

Other duties can be far ranging and potentially expose the individual directors to prosecution. Environmental, Health and Safety, Contractors, Regulators, even the most straightforward case may involve costs of £5-10k for representation costs.

HOWEVER, YOU NEED TO BE AWARE OF FOUR ACTS OF PARLIAMENT

1. HEALTH AND SAFETY AT WORK ACT 1974

Your corridors and stairwells are deemed to be a place of work.

Health and safety law places duties on MMM and directors can be personally liable when these duties are breached: members of the Board have both collective and individual responsibility for health and safety. If a health & safety offence is committed with the consent or connivance of, or is attributable to any neglect on the part of any director, manager, secretary or other similar officer of the organisation, then that person (as well as the organisation) can be prosecuted under s37.

You must take reasonable care to ensure the health and safety of anybody who will carry out work in your corridors, stairwells, roof, lift motor room, basement car park and common parts.

You can be prosecuted for dangerous practices started or continued with your consent, or illness or accidents attributable to your negligence.

2. CORPORATE MANSLAUGHTER AND CORPORATE HOMICIDE ACT 2007

An offence under this Act will be committed where failings by Directors are a substantial element in any gross breach of the duty of care owed to employees or members of the public, which results in death. In very extreme cases of wilful neglect or gross negligence a director could be convicted of manslaughter, which can carry a custodial sentence. The fines are unlimited and levied against the company not the Directors.

3. INSOLVENCY ACT 1986

Wrongful trading: You will be guilty of wrongful trading if you allow the business to carry on and incur debts when you know there is no reasonable prospect of repaying them. Can MMM pay its bills as and when they fall due? If not, you could be held personally liable for the company's debts if it subsequently becomes insolvent.

However, directors will not be made personally liable in circumstances where they can show they took every step prior to the liquidation to minimise the potential loss to the company's creditors.

A very important point: **Service Charges are neither an Asset nor a Liability of MMM.**

Unpaid service charges have no potential to be bad debts, as they are secured on property and a flat cannot be sold until the service charges are paid. So you will get your money eventually, but don't fall foul of the Limitation Act 1980. You must start legal action within six years.

The fact that a company is making **losses** does not in itself mean that the company is trading wrongfully. However, if MMM takes a lessee to the LVT and the lessee is successful with a s20C application, then you need to have thought out how the bills will be paid if they cannot be collected through the service charge. (see the Seventh Question).

Fraudulent trading: this occurs when a Director is knowingly a party to carrying on business with the intent to defraud the creditors. The courts may require that a director pays a contribution to the losses.

4. COMPANY DIRECTORS' DISQUALIFICATION ACT 1986

This Act might be relevant to you if you are a Company Director as part of your normal work. You would not want problems at MMM to bring an end to your career.

If you disagree with the decisions being made, you should have it noted in the minutes, including your reasons for disagreeing.

Is that all? Sadly not and a tribunal chairman recently remarked that after financial services, residential property management is now the second most highly regulated sector of the economy.

Do you employ Porters, Cleaners or Gardeners directly?

You must comply with **employment law** in dealings with employees.

You (personally) can be sued for unfair dismissal, discrimination or unfair work practices, such as unequal pay, so act quickly to ensure the Company complies with any new employment laws. Watch out for **legal pitfalls** in other areas: these include data protection, defamation, libel and providing misleading information.

Who employs the Porters?

A very good question and the standard answer is: *it depends who is asking the question.* Generally your managing agent will handle PAYE and NICs, so as far as HMRC is concerned, the Managing Agent is the Employer. However, the correct answer is generally that the Employer is MMM, the RMC or RTM Company.

FOURTH QUESTION: **DOES MY PRIVATE ADDRESS HAVE TO BE PUBLIC KNOWLEDGE?**

No. Companies House keeps Directors' private residential addresses confidential. Managing Agents prefer that your address at Companies House is their address, so that competitors cannot do mail shots to Directors.

Companies House has some useful guidance on its website about the situation after the 2006 Act and this is what they say:

Q. Will directors still have to provide their residential address to Companies House?

A. Yes. Every director must provide both their usual residential address and, for each directorship, a service address. The service address will be on the public record; the residential address will be protected information. A director may choose to use his residential address as his service address. If this is the case the service address will still appear on the public record, but the fact that the two addresses are the same will be protected information.

Q. Who will be able to obtain a directors' residential address from Companies House and why?

A. The following will be able to obtain directors' residential addresses:

- Specified public bodies for carrying out their public functions.
- Credit reference agencies for vetting applications for credit and associated work and to meet the obligations in the Money Laundering Regulations.
- Vulnerable directors will be able to apply to the Registrar for their addresses not to be provided to credit reference agencies.

Q. Which directors' addresses will not be provided to credit reference agencies?

A. Credit Reference agencies will not be able to obtain the usual residential address of any director who is the beneficiary of a valid Confidentiality Order on 30 September 2009 or who has made a successful application to the Registrar on the grounds that he is:

- at serious risk of violence or intimidation as a result of the activities of a company of which he is a director;
- or has been, employed by the police or security services;
- providing, or has provided, goods or services to the police or security services.

Q. If a company is in default, will any letter addressed to the directors go to the Service Address or residential address?

A. Letters will be sent to the Service Address.

Q. Can I remove my address from the register?

A. Generally once information has been placed on the public record it remains there in perpetuity. However, the Companies Act 2006 allows applications to be made to the Registrar to expunge an address from the public record where the availability of the address on the public record creates a risk of violence or intimidation. Please note that Companies House can only remove addresses that have been provided to the registrar since 2003.

Companies House says that the changes were made to meet four key objectives.

- To enhance shareholder engagement and a long term investment culture;
- To ensure better regulation and a 'Think Small First' approach;
- To make it easier to set up and run a company; and
- To provide flexibility for the future.

They have some more information on their website about the 2006 Act:

Q. Where can I get more information about the Companies Act 2006?

A. More information about the Companies Act 2006 is available on the Department for Business, Enterprise and Regulatory Reform website at http://www.berr.gov.uk/bbf/co-act-2006/index.html

Q. Is the Companies Act 2006 now complete?

A. No. The Act will be supplemented by a series of Regulations using powers given to the Secretary of State in certain parts of the Act. It will be supplemented by Commencement Orders which bring the Act into force. As they are published, details can be found at http://www.berr.gov.uk/bbf/co-act-2006/made-or-before-parliament/page35232.html

Q. What are the main changes in the Companies Act 2006?

A. Some of the key effects resulting from the Act include:

All companies:

- A clear statement of directors' general duties clarifies the existing case law based rules
- Companies are able to make greater use of electronic communications for communicating with shareholders.
- Directors can automatically have the option of filing a service address on the public record (rather than their private home address).
- Directors must be at least 16 years old and all companies must have one natural person as a director – i.e. they cannot have all corporate directors.
- There are improved rules for company names.
- Companies are no longer required to specify their objects on incorporation.
- The articles now form the basis of the company's constitution.

Private companies:

- There are separate and simpler model Articles of Association for private companies.
- As part of the "think small first" agenda, there is a separate, comprehensive "code" of accounting and reporting requirements for small companies.
- Private companies are not required to have a company secretary.
- Private companies do not need to hold an annual general meeting unless they positively opt to do so.
- It is easier for companies to take decisions by written resolutions.
- There are simpler rules on share capital, removing provisions that are largely irrelevant to the vast majority of private companies and their creditors.

Key benefits: Shareholders

- There are greater rights for nominee shareholders. These include the right to receive information electronically or in hard copy if they so wish.
- There is more timely accountability to shareholders by requiring public companies to hold their AGM within 6 months of the financial year-end.

For Private Companies the main relevant changes are:

There is now no need to appoint a Company Secretary

A Company Secretary is there to help with the administration associated with the running of your Company. Employing a Secretary relieves the Directors from much of the tedious routine work, such as maintaining the Company Books, issuing Share Certificates or Membership Certificates, ensuring compliance with filing requirements of Companies House and the Inland Revenue, sending out Notices of Meetings and so forth.

If you decide not to appoint a Company Secretary, somebody still has to carry out these tasks.

If your company was incorporated under the 1985 Companies Act then its Articles may require the appointment of a Secretary, so to benefit from this change you will have to amend the Articles. RTMs have no provision for a Secretary, but under Clause 10 the Directors can delegate powers to a Secretary.

This is what Companies House says:

Q. Do we still need a Company Secretary after April 2008?

A. From 6th April 2008 private companies have the option whether or not they have a company secretary.

Q. When did company secretary changes come into force?

A. On 6th April 2008 the provision for enabling private companies to choose whether they wish to have a company secretary, came into force.

Q. Can the company just have a sole director and no secretary?

A. Yes, as long as it is a private company and from 1st October 2008 that the director is a natural person (in other words, not an organisation).

Q. Must a secretary also be a natural person or can they be a corporate?

A. The new provisions relating to natural directors do not apply to secretaries. Secretaries can still be corporate.

Q. Is the company required to amend its Articles?

A. The company will be required to amend the Articles if there is specific reference to the company having a secretary. However if the Articles only refer to the secretary's duties there is no need to make an amendment.

Q. When the company amends the Articles what documentation must be submitted to Companies House?

A. The company must submit a written or special resolution together with an updated version of the Articles.

Q. When did the remaining provisions relating to secretaries come into force?

A. These came into force on 1st October 2009. From that date secretaries who are an individual person are able to file a service address for the public record and corporate secretaries are required to give details of where they are registered and the registered company number, if applicable.

There is now no need to hold an AGM

If you are an RTM then this will apply automatically, but for any other Company, if it is a requirement of your Mem & Arts to hold an AGM, then you will have to change these if you want to avoid this requirement.

However, it is a good idea to give all the lessees an opportunity once a year to get together to talk about the building, comment on the Budget and discuss policy issues for the future. Some buildings have a short formal meeting, then a general discussion, then a drink.

RTMs do not have a provision for the automatic retirement of Directors and re-election. There is no provision for the Board to remove an RTM Director, so the only way to control a couple of mavericks is to outnumber them on the Board or call a Company Meeting to remove them.

This is what the Companies House website says:

Q. Does my company still need to hold annual general meetings (AGMs)?

A. A private company does not need to hold an AGM if there is no obligation to do so in their articles. An existing company must continue to hold an AGM unless it changes its articles to remove any reference to AGMs. Public companies must still hold AGMs.

Q. What are the new provisions regarding AGMs (Annual General Meetings)

A. Under the Companies Act 2006 private companies will no longer be required to hold annual general meetings, however the shareholders will still be involved in the decision making process of the company.

The Act was drafted so many of these decisions can be made by written resolution, although the company will still need to hold meetings to dismiss a director or remove an auditor before the end of the term of office. The shareholders and directors also still have the power to call a meeting, if required.

The effect of the new provisions is dependent on what is currently in a company's articles. An existing private company would still need to pass a resolution to remove any existing clauses regarding annual general meetings from its articles. Notice of this resolution would be circulated to the members before it could be passed or agreed to.

There are Changes to the Rules on Meetings and Resolutions

Again, if you are not an RTM you may have to change your Articles to have the benefit of some of these changes.

This is what the Companies House Website says:

Q. After 1st October 2007 does a company still need to hold an extraordinary general meeting (EGM) to pass an extraordinary resolution?

A. After 1st October 2007 a company will only have to hold an EGM to pass an extraordinary resolution if it is stated in the company's articles.

Q. Has the 2006 Act removed the requirement to pass an extraordinary resolution?

A. Yes, for example the Insolvency Act 1986 stated a company had to pass an extraordinary resolution to wind up a company. This is no longer the case as a consequential amendment has been made to the Insolvency Act 1986 to change the requirement from an extraordinary resolution to a special resolution.

Q. Can any resolution that was passed as an extraordinary resolution under the Companies Act 1985 now be passed as a special resolution?

A. Yes.

Q. Following the 1st October 2007 are there any wording or requirements changes for passing special / written resolutions?

A. Companies House would expect the resolution to state: the resolution type, the fact it was passed / agreed by the members or directors, the date it was passed and it has been signed by an officer of the company.

Q. When did Part 13 on resolutions come into force?

A. 1st October 2007

Q. What is the required majority needed for written resolutions?

A. The required majority will be similar to that for shareholders' meetings – a simple majority of eligible shares for ordinary resolutions, or more for special resolutions.

Q. Do written resolutions need to be signed by each of the individuals named on the resolution?

A. Written resolutions passed on or after 1 October 2007 (under the Companies Act 2006) require only one signature (but may have more).

Q. Will proposed written resolutions have to be notified to the auditors?

A. Yes, Section 390 of the Companies Act 1985 will be amended so that auditors are still entitled to receive all communications that go to members in connection with written resolutions.

Q. Does my company still need to hold annual general meetings (AGM's)?

A. A private company does not need to hold an AGM if there is no obligation to do so in their articles. An existing company must continue to hold an AGM unless it changes it's articles to remove any reference to AGM's. Public companies must still hold AGM's.

Q. What is the notice period for shareholders meetings?

A. Shareholder meetings for private companies can now all be on a 14 day notice period, unless different arrangements are specified in a company's articles.

Q. Have elective resolutions been repealed?

A. Under the Companies Act 2006 elective resolutions excluding section 80a (now section 549-55 of the 2006 Act) have been repealed.

As of 1 October 2007, four of the five elective resolution types are no longer necessary to be filed for private limited companies - these being:

- Dispensing with the laying of accounts and reports before a general meeting (s252)
- Dispensing with the holding of annual general meetings (s366a)
- Reduction of majority required to authorise a meeting at short notice (s369(4) or 378(3))
- Dispensing with the annual appointment of auditors (s386)

But if they are filed they will be placed on the public record.

Q. Does a company have to pass a resolution to use a website as a way of members seeing accounts?

A. Firstly, the company must check the current articles to see what is specified and if they wish to take advantage of not having to hold an AGM they must pass a resolution to remove that provision. However they may continue to present the accounts to members as they currently do.

Q. If the company doesn't change its articles is this against company law?

A. This is not compulsory. The company articles will only need to change if a company wants to take advantage of the new provisions which came into force on 1st October 2007, e.g. directors' duties, resolutions and meetings.

Q. Can a company adopt a completely new set of articles if a member does not agree with one part?

A. If the company passes a special resolution to adopt a bespoke set of articles, at least 75% of the eligible votes are required. Therefore, it will depend on how many eligible votes that company has (i.e. how many members).

Further detailed information on resolutions and meetings is contained within Companies Act 2006: Private Company Information, on the BIS website: http://www.bis.gov.uk/files/file42261.pdf

What is the difference between a Special, Ordinary and Extraordinary Resolution?

An Ordinary Resolution is used for all matters unless the Companies Act or the company's articles of association require another type of resolution. Ordinary Resolutions are passed by a simple majority, Special Resolutions require a minimum 75% majority.

Special Resolutions are required for important matters such as alterations to the memorandum or articles of association, a change of name, or a reduction of capital to be approved by the court.

Since October 2007, a company has been required to hold an extraordinary general meeting to pass an extraordinary resolution only if it is stated in its articles. Any resolution that was passed as an extraordinary resolution under the Companies Act 1985 can now be passed as a special resolution.

There are changes to the right of access to the Register of Members

You do not have to give out a List of Company Members to anybody who asks for it, but you do have to allow certain people to view it at the Registered Office.

This is what Companies House says:

Q. When will it be possible for a company to be relieved from the statutory obligation to allow anyone access to its register of members?

A. Once a company has filed its Annual Return made up to a date after 30 September 2007, it will be subject to the 2006 Act's provisions relating to access to its register of members. This means that:

- the request for access must include the name and address of the persons seeking access and say what the information is to be used for, whether it will be shared with anyone else and if so, to whom and for what purpose;
- the company must, within five working days, either comply with the request for access or apply to the court;
- the court will allow the company not to comply if it is satisfied that the access is not being sought for a proper purpose.

Q. Who does the restriction to the register of members apply to?

A. This restriction applies to all external requests to view the register of members from outside the company.

Q. As a result of a request to see the register of members what information can the company ask for?

A. The requester's name and address, or if an organisation an individual's name, plus the purpose of the request and whether the information will be shared with anyone else and if so, to whom and for what purpose. It is an offence to make a false statement when providing the details required for disclosure.

Q. What options does the company have with regards to disclosure of the register of members information?

A. The company must, within 5 working days, either comply with the request or apply to the court to restrict the access to the Register.

Q. When would the court allow the company not to comply with the request for access?

A. The court would only allow the company not to comply if it is satisfied that the access is not being sought for a proper purpose.

Q. What is a proper purpose for access to a company's register of members?

A. It is for the court to determine whether any particular application is for a proper purpose.

The **Registered Office** is the official address to which all Company correspondence is directed. Although Companies House must be kept advised of the Directors' current residential addresses, this information is kept private. Directors can choose only to display their address in public as "The Company's Registered Office".

This is what Companies House says:

Q. What is a registered office address?

A. All companies must have a registered office, which must be situated at a physical location in their country of registration. It can be a business address, the address of a managing agent or accountant or any other address the company chooses. However, it must be an address at which the company will be able to deal with all official letters and notices that are received.

Q. Can a PO Box be used for the registered office address?

A. Yes, provided the full physical address is given including the postcode.

Do you have Headed Paper for MMM?

If so, remember that you must put the Registered Number, where Registered and the Registered Office on the notepaper somewhere. If you list Directors' names, you can either list all of them or none of them, but you cannot be selective on who you miss out.

All companies using a website and emails must put on them the same information as required on the letter headed paper.

There is more room to take decisions by written resolution, requiring a simple majority (ordinary resolution) or at least 75% of eligible votes (special resolution). Previously, written resolutions required unanimity. There are now simpler rules on accounting and reporting.

Right to Manage Companies

The new Act automatically applies to RTMs, since the Articles are prescribed by Statute.

The RTM Companies (Model Articles) (England) Regulations 2009(SI 2009/2767) introduced model Articles for RTMCos formed on or after 9 November 2009.

From 1 October 2010 the new Articles take effect for all RTMCos formed before 9 November 2009 whether or not they are formally adopted. Right to manage is particular to leasehold flats and maisonettes, but not to leasehold houses or estates. Different regulations apply in Wales but the effect is the same.

SIXTH QUESTION: WHAT SHOULD I BE LOOKING FOR IN THE COMPANY ACCOUNTS?

The Company and the Building are quite different entities. The Company has to have Company Accounts and the Building has to have Service Charge Accounts. There are entirely different regulatory regimes and the service charge funds are neither an asset nor a liability of the Company. The Service Charge funds are held on trust for the lessees.

Does the Company have any income?

Your Company may own the freehold and so may collect Ground Rents. These are taxable, but you will have expenditure to offset against this, such as accountants' fees, filing fees, postage and administration costs.

What happens if the Company has no income? We deal with this increasingly important question in the next section, but where the building is running smoothly it is traditional to:

- Take the Company Administration and Running Costs as Service Charge Expenditure
- File Dormant Accounts with Companies House and
- Apply to HMRC for five years exemption from making Corporation Tax returns

You will then only produce Service Charge Accounts and would normally have these Certified by an external accountant. The lease may say an 'audit' is required, but an audit to international standards is very expensive and in such cases it is general practice to have the accounts Certified unless a lessee requires otherwise.

If the lease says nothing about external certification and there are more than four flats in the building, then you could decide to wait for a lessee to serve a s21 Notice under the Landlord and Tenant Act 1985 before doing an audit or certification. However, you only get 30 days to do it, so generally a Board will want to have some form of external third party verification simply to protect their own position.

Having said that, the sanctions for not complying with a s21 Notice are uncertain. The last time we asked we were told that only two Local Authorities in the country would currently take action following a complaint.

If you obtain substantial bank interest on your service charge deposits, depending on the lease, these would normally be Service Charge funds, not income of the RMC or RTM Company. You will need to file a Trust Tax Return, but if the bank deducts tax from the interest and the total in the year is less than £1,000 you can get exemption from making a return.

Here is some advice from ICAEW TECHNICAL RELEASE – TECH 03/11

Banking arrangements for service charge monies

The following is a summary of the best practice in this guidance.

- If the lease/tenancy agreement sets out the way in which service charges are to be accounted for, who shall certify or approve the accounts, the costs that can be recovered and the periods of time for which accounts should be prepared, then the requirements of the lease must be followed.
- Service charge monies paid by lessees are trust monies and should be held in ring fenced designated bank accounts (s42, Landlord and Tenant Act 1987).
- A landlord or managing agent need not have a separate bank account for each property/scheme unless the lease requires one. But the funds for each property or scheme must be separately identifiable as it is a breach of trust to use service charge monies from one property/scheme to pay the bills of another or of the landlord.

- All lessees paying variable service charges should receive an annual service charge statement from their landlord or residents' management company (RMC) (including right to manage companies (RTM)) within six months of the end of the accounting year.
- The annual statement should include an income and expenditure account and a balance sheet and be prepared on an accruals basis.
- All annual statements of account should be subject to an examination by an independent accountant before issue to lessees.
- This Technical Release provides guidance on the two alternative types of examination that may be undertaken by the independent accountant depending upon the terms of the lease. The type of engagement, which should be agreed between the accountant and the client landlord, RMC or their agent, will depend on the terms of the lease and should be proportionate to the size and nature of the property/scheme.
- If the service charge statement is prepared on behalf of an RMC or RTM then it should be a separate statement to the annual accounts for the company required to be filed at Companies House.

How do we make a Trust Tax Return?

The guidance on the HMRC website is under Corporation Tax. Go to Charities, Organisations and Tax Agents and then under that Unincorporated Organisations and Corporation Tax and at the bottom you will see the guidance on Property Management Companies.

Tax for Trusts (the interest you get on your bank deposit account) is handled by:

Trusts & Estates
Ferrers House
Castle Meadow Road
Nottingham NG2 1BB

Telephone: 0845 604 6455

HMRC have confirmed that *"if no trust record is held then HMRC do not need to be advised of its existence if the taxable income is under £1,000."* So if you do not have a Unique Taxpayer Reference (UTR) for the bank account in question, HMRC are only interested in hearing from you when the interest goes over £1,000. On the other hand, they may write to you first with a UTR, in which case you will have to make a return.

Where the Landlord is an **RMC** or **RTM** or similar company, service charge monies are subject to a statutory trust. Trust monies do not belong to the RMC/RTM and so should not be included as an asset in the **statutory accounts** of the RMC/RTM.

Section 42, LTA 1987 requires service charge monies from variable service charges to be held in trust(except for social landlords). It does not specify what this would mean in practice. Although s42,LTA 1987 does not explicitly require service charge monies to be held in a separate trust or 'client' bank account, it does impose a statutory trust on the person to whom service charges are paid and that person will be liable for any breach of the trust. For example if service charge monies are held in the bank account of the RMC or RTM, they may be taken as the company's assets in any liquidation following a company insolvency and the directors of the company could be personally liable for the breach of trust.

The RICS Service Charge Residential Management Code ('The Code') sets out what is best practice for all landlords, managing agents, RMCs and RTMs. Part 10.8 states that service charge funds for each property should be identifiable and either be placed in a separate bank account, or in a single client/trust account where the accounting records separately identify the fund attributable to each property.

It is therefore best practice for landlords or their agents to open a separate bank account for each property/development. That bank account should have the word 'trust' or 'client' or the name of the property in its title. For example "Magnificent Mansions Trust Account."There is no requirement in the Code to open separate bank accounts for reserve funds apart from current service charge monies unless the lease requires it or a client/landlord prefers this arrangement.

Some Legal Points

One of the points on which legal opinion has been obtained by the ICAEW is:

What are the consequences of service charge monies' being held on trust?

Q. Who is or are the trustees?

A. The legal payee is the trustee. The legal payee will be the RMC if it is 'the landlord or other person to whom any such charges are payable by those tenants ... under the terms of their leases' as defined in s42(1), LTA 1987. The legal payee is the landlord even if the service charges are physically paid to another person, for example a managing agent.

Q. Does the existence of an express, implied or statutory trust establish the service charge fund as a separate entity?

A. The trust fund is a pool of money: it has no separate legal personality.

Q. Does the existence of an express, implied or statutory trust result in the company's having the ability to 'deploy' but not the ability to 'enjoy' service charge monies?

A. Yes. The company does have the ability to 'deploy' but not to 'enjoy' the funds under its control.

SEVENTH QUESTION:
WHAT HAPPENS IF WE LOSE A CASE AT THE LEASEHOLD VALUATION TRIBUNAL?

A very good question. As we noted above, MMM probably has no income, so it has no funds with which to pay any expenses or awards of a Court or Tribunal.

There may be a built-in problem, such as the leases in total do not recover 100% of the expenditure, or you cannot recover through the lease the costs of chasing service charge arrears. Arrears of Service Charge are not generally a long-term problem as they can be recovered on a sale, but you will need to start legal action even for a small amount within six years or risk falling foul of the Limitation Act 1980.

ARMA in their Guidance Note suggest that the Board should consider a levy on shareholders. It is also suggested that Companies should consider changing their Mem & Arts to enable a call on shareholders to be made by Special Resolution or by the Board. You could also insert a clause in the articles to allow an annual membership fee.

If you want to investigate these options, you should get legal advice.

Care should be taken to ensure that directors do not incur costs frivolously at a cost to shareholders.

There are four possible areas where you could consider creating income for the RMC or RTM:

- A Management Fee charged by the Board for its services under the lease
- Insurance Commissions
- Administration Charges for dealing with lease issues on behalf of the freeholder
- Charges for services that fall outside the lease provisions. Much will depend on circumstances, but you might be able to charge for: use of lockable cycle storage racks, car parking, additional TV services, window cleaning, shared flat internal security alarm systems, flat cleaning. Any cost recharges would include a generous mark-up for the Company.

Any income will be taxable at corporation tax rates, but you can offset company expenditure. You can collect in funds to build up a Reserve without incurring corporation tax. You might decide to wait for a need, borrow to pay for it and then think about a way to repay it. Or you might prefer to Be Prepared, open a separate Company bank account and put something in it.

RTM Companies have two special problems: (a) not all lessees may be members and (b) the Articles are prescribed by Statute and cannot be changed.

On this second point it should be noted:

i. The RTM Articles assume the Company will have some income but it is not clear where the Government thinks this will come from
ii. It must be assumed that the Company will generate enough income to pay the administration costs of the Company (filing fees, accountants' fees)

Watch the Property Press for creative solutions being put up and whether the LVT or Upper Tribunal knock them down.

EIGHTH QUESTION: **WHAT IS TABLE A?**

This is relevant if your company was formed under the Companies Act 1985 or previous Acts.

Table A is simply the name given to the prescribed format for Articles of Association of a company limited by shares under the Companies Act 1985 and earlier legislation. The Articles set out the regulations by which the company will be managed.

Why would I need to refer to a "Table A"?

When a company limited by shares is incorporated, it does not need to file Articles if it wishes to use Table A as its Articles. In this case, if you search the records of a company limited by shares you may not find a document setting out its Articles. Certain provisions of Table A may also apply to a company which has filed Articles, if the company's Articles have not specifically excluded or modified Table A. In either case, if you want to see the regulations that govern the management of the company, you need to refer to the relevant Table A.

Which Table A is relevant to a particular company?

The Table A which applies to a company is the Table A in force at the date of the company's incorporation. If Table A was subsequently altered, the changes do not affect a company registered before the alteration took effect. To be sure you are reading the correct Table A, you need to know the date of incorporation of the company and which version of Table A was in force on that date.

The first prescribed format of Articles was made in "The Joint Stock Companies Act, 1856". In this Act, the Articles were called "Table B" (simply because they were preceded by a form of Memorandum of Association called "Form A"). At the next prescription, which happened in 1862, the Memorandum was moved into the body of the Act and the Articles became "Table A". This naming convention for the Articles continued through legislation introduced in 1906, 1908, 1929, 1948 (and amendments made in 1967, 1976, 1980, 1981) and July 1985 (and amendments made in August 1985 and 2000) and in 2007.

The following list shows the effective date of each Table A.

The effective date of each Table A	
Table A prescribed by:	**Effective from:**
Joint Stock Companies Act 1856 (Table B)	14 July 1856
The Companies Act 1862	7 August 1862
Board of Trade Order 1906	1 October 1906
Companies Consolidation Act 1908	1 April 1909
Companies Act 1929	1 November 1929
Companies Act 1948	1 July 1948
- as amended by Companies Act 1967	27 January 1968
- as amended by Companies Act 1976 (3 commencement dates)	18 April 1977, 1 June 1977 and 1 October 1977
- as amended by the Stock Exchange (Completion of Bargains) Act 1976 Part 1 - as amended by the Stock Exchange (Completion of Bargains) Act 1976 Part 2 - as amended by the Stock Exchange (Completion of Bargains) Act 1976 Part 3	2 February 1979
- as amended by Companies Act 1980	22 December 1980
- as amended by Companies Act 1981	3 December 1981
Companies (Tables A to F) Regulations 1985	1 July 1985
- as amended by Companies (Tables A to F) (Amendment) Regulations 1985	1 August 1985
- as amended by Companies Act 1985 (Electronic Communications) Order 2000	22 December 2000
- as amended by Companies (Tables A to F) (Amendment) Regulations 2007 and The Companies (Tables A to F) (Amendment) (No. 2) Regulations 2007 for private companies limited by shares	1 October 2007
- as amended by Companies (Tables A to F) (Amendment) Regulations 2007 and The Companies (Tables A to F) (Amendment) (No. 2) Regulations 2007 for public companies limited by shares	

Q. What if I want to resign as a Director?

If you wish to resign as a Director then you do not have to wait until a General Meeting to do so. You can resign at any time, however it is polite to let the other Members of the Board know beforehand so they can if necessary invite others to take your place.

This is especially relevant if you are selling and will cease to be eligible to act as a Director on completion.

If you are the last remaining Director and you choose to resign, then this will leave the Company in difficulty and you may be in breach of your duties as a director in doing so. The same is true if you were one of two Directors and the Articles of Association stipulate the minimum number of Directors is two.

Q. What if nobody stands as a Director?

Under the 2006 Companies Act a Company can function with only one Director and no other Officers, however if your Company pre-dates it then the Articles of Association may stipulate a minimum number of Directors which may be two. Provision is often made for a single Director to do what is necessary to appoint a second Director, but (s)he is often prevented from doing anything else in the meantime.

If the last remaining Director resigns, then the Company cannot function and will ultimately be struck off. This can be extremely problematic for flat owners. In the case where a Company owns the freehold, the freehold may revert to the Crown and you will have to contact the Treasury Solicitor to buy it back. Whether or not the Company owns the Freehold, in the shorter term if it is struck off, this can be a difficulty for any owner wishing to sell.

Q. How do I stop MMM being Hijacked?

In most cases Companies House may not cross-check the signatures on hard copy forms. This means there is a risk that your Company could be hijacked by an individual who uses an invalid countersignature on his appointment form AP01.

It is possible to prevent this by registering your Company with Companies House for protected online filing (PROOF). This means that only forms submitted electronically will be accepted. All electronic filings are protected by a unique secure filing code, which acts as a PIN. Notification of the secure filing code is kept at the registered office.

TENTH QUESTION:
ALRIGHT, I'M PERSUADED: HOW DO I GET APPOINTED AS A DIRECTOR?

In general, there are two ways of being appointed as a Director: either the existing Board can appoint you as a new Director at any time or else you can be appointed at a General Meeting of the Company's Members.

If you are appointed by the existing Board on a casual basis, then your appointment will need to be endorsed at the next General Meeting. **You cannot be appointed without your consent.** Either you will be asked to complete and sign a paper form AP01 or else your appointment can be filed electronically at Companies House using 3 confidential items of personal information to verify your identity.

If you sign consenting to be a Director on a hard copy AP01 then your form will need to be countersigned by an existing Officer of the Company. If your AP01 is filed electronically, then the Company's secure filing code will be used to confirm that you are appointed with the consent of the Board.

RULE 1   Know your authority and don't exceed it

All RMC Directors should equip themselves with a copy of the Memorandum and Articles of Association of the Company in order that they know its objects and the powers of the Board. Also ensure you get a letter of appointment which makes clear the terms upon which you are appointed and the extent to which you will be expected to participate in the business of the Company. Every Director should have a full appreciation of the extent to which the Company and its Board are governed by the general law as well as having a working knowledge of the lease.

RULE 2   Act reasonably and openly

The reasonable Director can do no wrong. What is reasonable will be determined with 20:20 hindsight, possibly by someone who does not necessarily have the interests of the reasonable Director at heart. Accordingly, err on the side of caution and always disclose any other interests particularly where they may conceivably – however remotely – give rise to a conflict with the interests of the Company.

RULE 3   Delegate don't abdicate

Be fully aware of the structure of the RMC or RTM. Ensure that Agents have clear lines of responsibility and that there is adequate provision for succession on your Board.

RULE 4   Ensure adequate systems for compliance

Board meetings must be held regularly for which full agendas and working papers should be provided. Give consideration to the content of the agenda. As well as financial information, there are a number of additional areas which the Board of every Company should review regularly. Examples are health and safety, fire risk assessment and insurance and the relevant list will depend upon the circumstances of each individual RMC or RTM.

RULE 5   Keep well informed and maintain good records

No major decision should be taken by any Board without the Secretary circulating a paper beforehand reviewing the subject thoroughly. Every Director should ensure that proper Board Minutes are maintained showing how decisions were taken and who participated in them. Each Director should keep – for an appropriate period – copies of relevant Board papers. Do not try and facilitate informal discussions outside Board Meetings particularly on strategic issues which should only be brought to the Board through a formal Board paper.

RULE 6   Don't dispose of assets at an undervalue

Where relevant, you may require a professional valuation before selling or transferring an asset and where a professional valuation is inappropriate you should probe for the reasons and basis for such transactions.

RULE 7   Don't mislead creditors

Major creditors, for example banks, should be kept regularly informed. Indeed it is a common contractual requirement to do so under the provisions of loan agreements. It goes without saying that no creditors, large or small, should be misled at any time.

RULE 8   Review regularly the Company's capacity to trade

Full financial information incorporating at least twelve months cash flow should be regularly produced and updated. All Directors and not just the one looking after finances should ask to see any bank facility letters. If difficult financial circumstances arise, act reasonably. Any rescue plan must be realistic. Ask yourself the question: is the position of the generality of creditors made better or worse by continuing to trade?

RULE 9   Take out insurance

Ensure that the Company's insurance is adequate both as to the scope and amount of cover for your RMC's or RTM's circumstances. In addition ensure that the Company insures all Directors for Directors' and Officers' liability, but check first to see whether the cost should be a service charge item authorised by the lease. If it is not, then make it a corporate expense and pay from corporate funds.

RULE 10 Seek professional advice early

This should be done for its own sake because it is often cheaper to consult professional advisers early. "A stitch in time saves nine" may be a trite saying, but it frequently has application to management matters. In addition, seeking professional advice early serves to establish reasonableness as decided in many of the Insolvency Act cases.

SOME TIPS WE WOULD ADD FROM OUR EXPERIENCE

• Make sure you have a good Managing Agent

• Check your Managing Agent is on top of the numbers on a monthly basis and has financial reporting systems you can access easily

• If you self manage, get a third party to do your service charge collection and debt collection to avoid unpleasantness with people you live with

• Check insurances regularly and watch out for expiry dates

• Make sure you have a range of relevant expertise between Board members and if not, actively look for a lessee who is a builder or a surveyor, or has accounting or legal knowledge, or whatever expertise or experience you feel you lack as a team

• You must always consider the interests of other stakeholders such as creditors and employees; you must consider the long-term prospects of the Company and its reputation; you must give equal consideration to all shareholders.

• In exercising directors' powers, you are required to exhibit 'such a degree of skill as may reasonably be expected' from a person with your knowledge and experience. For example, a chartered accountant might be expected to know if the Company was trading whilst insolvent.

• You must also exercise a degree of care in your actions as a Director: the test of an acceptable level of care is what a reasonable person would do in looking after their own affairs.

• You are generally not liable for the actions of your fellow directors, if you knew nothing about them and took no part in them, but you have a duty to make sure you are informed about the Company's affairs. It is very dangerous to turn a blind eye.

• Talk to people in the building when you bump into them so you can keep your ear to the ground and head off potential problems before they arise

• Think about conflicts of interest when you make suggestions or recommend anybody

• Avoid asking contractors or porters for favours

• Have a highlighted copy of the lease with you at Board Meetings

• When in doubt, get professional help paid for through the service charge account, but check the lease

• Be ready to justify your decisions as a Board to a Leasehold Valuation Tribunal

• Keep an ongoing Property Maintenance Plan updated on a regular basis so that the Reserve Fund collections are adequate and the Building does not run out of cash, or need to make extra cash calls on lessees

• Make sure each year you review the Health & Safety Report and Fire Risk Assessment

APPENDIX 1: **ANALYSING YOUR ARTICLES OF ASSOCIATION**

A Right to Manage Company	Your Company
The Objects of the Company	
5 it can employ staff and managing agents	
it can set up reserve funds	
it can lend money or give credit or guarantees	
it can borrow money	
Liability of the Members	
7 Limited to £1	
Directors' Powers & Responsibilities	
9 Members can by special resolution direct the Directors to do or not do something	
However, this cannot be retrospective	
10 Directors may delegate to a person or a committee as they think fit and then revoke it	
11 Any Committees must follow procedures based on the Articles	
Directors Decision Making	
12 The general rule is that decisions must be either a majority decision at a meeting or a unanimous decision agreed in writing or signed by all eligible directors	
If there is only one director, this can be ignored	
14 Any director may call a Board meeting by giving notice, which must include (a) the proposed date and time and place and (b) how directors not in the place will participate during the meeting.	
Notice must be given, but need not be in writing	
Notice need not be given to directors who waive their entitlement to notice not more than seven days after the date of the meeting.	
16 The quorum for a Board meeting can be fixed from time to time, but must never be less than two and if not fixed by the directors is to be two.	
Without a quorum, the only decisions that can be made are (a) to call another meeting (b) to appoint more directors and (c) to call a general meeting to appoint more directors.	
17 The directors may appoint a chairman and can terminate this appointment at any time.	
If the chairman does not arrive within ten minutes of the start, the directors must appoint one of them to chair the meeting.	
18 The chairman has a casting vote, unless the chairman is not allowed to vote on the issue.	
Conflicts of Interest	
19 A Director with an interest in a decision cannot vote, unless (a) the interest cannot reasonably be regarded as likely to give rise to a conflict of interest or (b) the conflict of interest arises from a permitted cause (such as a guarantee, a subscription for securities, or arrangements for benefits).	
The Company by ordinary resolution can allow a director with a conflict of interest to vote.	
If there is a dispute about the right of a director to vote, the chairman has to make a ruling.	
If the director whose right to vote is disputed is the chairman, then all the directors (excluding the chairman) will vote on it.	
Recording Decisions	
20 The directors must ensure that records of decisions are kept in writing for at least ten years from the date of the decision.	
Writing means the representation or reproduction of words in a visible form by any method whether sent or supplied in electronic form or otherwise.	

21 Subject to the Articles, the Directors may make any rule which they think fit about how they make and record decisions.

Appointment of Directors

22 Any willing person can be appointed by ordinary resolution or a decision of the directors.

If all the members and directors die, the personal representatives of the last member to have died have the right to appoint a person a director.

If the last two die at the same time, the younger is deemed to have survived the older.

23 A person stops being a director if (a) they are no longer qualified under the Acts (b) if they have a bankruptcy order made against them (c) a composition is made with creditors (d) a doctor says in writing the person is physically or mentally incapable of acting as a director and may remain so for more than three months or (e) the director resigns.

24 Directors are not entitled to remuneration unless the Company consents in general meeting.

25 The company may pay reasonable expenses for attendance at meetings of directors, general meetings, meetings with debenture holders or otherwise in connection with the exercise of their powers and the discharge of their responsibilities.

Becoming and Ceasing to be a Member

26 Every person entitled to be and wanting to be a member must give the Company a signed application form.

The only people who can be members are (a) a qualifying tenant of a flat or (b) the landlord, but only after the date of acquisition.

Membership is not transferable.

Joint owners of flats are a joint member in respect of the flat.

The directors when satisfied about the application and entitlement shall register the person as a member.

27 If a person ceases to satisfy the requirements for membership they cease to be a member with immediate effect.

If a member or joint member dies or becomes bankrupt, his personal representatives or trustee are entitled to be registered as a member or joint member upon notice in writing.

A member may withdraw by giving seven clear days' notice in writing, unless this is during the period between the Notice of Claim and the Acquisition Date or the withdrawal of the Notice.

If a person becomes a joint qualifying tenant but fails to apply for membership within 28 days, or if personal representatives or trustees do not apply within 56 days, or if a member resigns, then membership ceases with immediate effect, but all these people are entitled to re-apply for membership.

Organisation of General Meetings

28 In determining attendance at a General Meeting, it is immaterial whether any two or more members attending it are in the same place as each other.

The Directors may make whatever arrangements they consider appropriate to enable those attending a general meeting to exercise their rights to speak or vote at it.

No business, apart from appointing a chairman, can be transacted if there is no quorum.

29 The quorum shall be 20% of the members of the company entitled to vote upon the business to be transacted, or two members of the company (whichever is greater), present in person or by proxy.

30 If the chairman has not arrived within ten minutes of the start, the directors present or (if none present) the meeting must appoint a chairman and this must be the first business of the meeting.

31 Directors may attend and speak at general meetings, whether or not they are members.

The chairman may permit non-members to attend and speak.

32   If there is no quorum within 30 minutes, the chairman must adjourn the meeting.

The chairman may adjourn a meeting with a quorum if (a) the meeting consents or (b) it appears to the chairman it is necessary to protect the safety of any person, or ensure the business is conducted in an orderly manner.

The chairman must adjourn a meeting if directed to do so by the meeting.

When adjourning a meeting, the chairman must either specify the time and place to which it is adjourned or state that it is to continue at a time and place to be fixed by the directors. He must have regard to any directions given by the meeting.

If the continuation of an adjourned meeting is to be more than 14 days after the adjournment, the company must give at least 7 clear days' notice to the same persons containing the same information required by such a notice.

Voting at General Meetings

33   A resolution put to the vote must be decided on a show of hands unless a poll is duly demanded.

If there are no landlords who are members, then it is one vote per flat.

If there are non-residential areas in the building, then the number of votes they have is based on floor area as set out in 33(3)(b).

The Landlord is not entitled to a vote for a flat whose qualifying tenant is not a member.

If a flat does not have a lease, it does not have a vote.

A landlord who is a member is entitled to one vote.

If two or more joint members try to vote, the vote of the senior only shall be accepted and seniority is defined as the order in which the names of the persons appear in the register of members in respect of the flat or lease.

Errors and Disputes

34   Objections to the qualification of any person voting may only be made at the meeting and every vote not disallowed at the meeting is valid.

Any objections must be referred to the chairman whose decision is final.

Poll Votes

35   A poll on a resolution can be demanded in advance of the general meeting, or at the meeting before or after the show of hands.

A poll can be demanded by the chairman, the directors, two or more people entitled to vote, or the representative(s) of not less than 10% of those entitled to vote.

A demand for a poll can be withdrawn if the poll has not yet been taken and the chairman consents.

Polls must be taken immediately and in the way the chairman directs.

Proxy Notices

36   Valid proxies can only be appointed by a written notice stating the name and address of the member appointing the proxy, identifying the person appointed and the meeting for which the proxy is appointed. It must be signed by the member, or authenticated by the directors and delivered in accordance with the articles and instructions contained in the notice of the meeting to which they relate.

The company may require proxy notices to be delivered in a particular form and may specify different forms for different purposes.

Proxy notices may specify how the proxy is to vote (or abstain) on one or more resolutions.

Unless the proxy notice indicates otherwise, it must be treated as allowing the proxy discretion on ancillary or procedural resolutions and the proxy extends to any adjournment.

37   A person entitled to attend, speak or vote remains entitled to do so at the meeting even if a valid proxy notice has been given.

A proxy notice can be revoked by delivering to the company a notice in writing.

A notice revoking a proxy appointment only takes effect if it is delivered before the meeting or adjourned meeting.

If a proxy notice is not executed by the person appointing the proxy, it must be accompanied by written evidence of the authority of the person who executed it.

Amendments to Resolutions

38 An ordinary resolution to be proposed may be amended by ordinary resolution if notice is given to the company in writing by a person entitled to vote not less than 48 hours before the meeting and the proposed amendment does not, in the reasonable opinion of the chairman, materially alter the scope of the resolution.

A special resolution to be proposed may be amended by ordinary resolution if the chairman proposes it and the amendment does not go beyond what is necessary to correct a grammatical or other non-substantive error in the resolution.

If the chairman, acting in good faith, wrongly declares that an amendment is out of order, the chairman's error does not invalidate the vote.

Administrative Arrangements

39 Subject to the Articles, anything sent or supplied by or to the company may be sent or supplied as provided in the Companies Acts.

Subject to the Articles, any notice or document sent to a director may be sent in the way the director asks.

A director may agree that notices or documents sent in a particular way are deemed to have been received within a specified time of their being sent and that time can be less than 48 hours.

40 Any common seal may only be used by the authority of the directors and the directors may decide how this is to be done.

Unless otherwise decided, if the company uses the seal, the document must be signed by at least one authorised person in the presence of a witness who attests the signature. An authorised person means (a) a director (b) the company secretary (if any) or (c) any person authorised by the directors.

41 Any member shall have the right on reasonable notice at such time or place convenient for the company, to inspect and be provided with a copy of any book, minute, document or accounting record of the company, upon payment of a reasonable copying charge,

If there is confidential material the disclosure of which would be contrary to the best interests of the company, then this can be excluded but the fact of the exclusion must be made known to the member. The directors can set reasonable conditions on disclosure.

42 The directors can make provision for the benefit of employees in connection with the cessation or transfer of the whole or part of the undertaking of the company,

Directors' Indemnity and Insurance

43 A director or former director may be indemnified out of the company's assets against (a) any liability incurred by the director in connection with any negligence, default, breach of duty or breach of trust (b) any liability in connection with the activities of the company as a trustee of an occupational pension scheme (c) any other liability incurred by that director as an officer of the company.

However, this article does not authorise any indemnity which would be prohibited or rendered void by any provision of the Companies Acts or by any other provision of law.

44 The directors may decide to purchase insurance, at the expense of the company, for the benefit of any director or former director in respect of any relevant loss.

A 'relevant loss' means any loss or liability incurred in connection with the director's duties or powers in relation to the company.

APPENDIX 2: **KEY POINTS TO LOOK FOR IN YOUR LEASE**

Does your lease include these? If not, what are the implications for your building?

- the right to collect a Reserve Fund

- the right to transfer service charge surpluses to the Reserve Fund

- the right to collect all costs both legal and Managing Agents for breaches of the lease

- service charges to be collected in advance

- the financial year end to be at the Landlord's discretion

- administration fees to be 'reasonable' and not a fixed sum

- the right to charge to the lessee legal, Managing Agent's and Debt Collection agency costs as part of the cost of recovery of arrears even if no Section 146 Notice is issued to the lessee and the right to charge such costs and Tribunal costs if necessary to the Service Charge account

- interest to be charged on late payment of ground rents, service charges and all other charges recoverable under the lease

- not to use the flat for work

- occupation should be by one 'family' only

- sub-lettings to require Landlord's approval

- no short or holiday lets are allowed

- the Landlord has the right to make regulations for the better management of the building

- no pets without written permission from the Landlord or Managing Agent, permission to be revocable at any time at the Landlord's complete discretion

- no absolute obligation on the Landlord to clean the windows

- an obligation on the lessee to maintain bath and shower seals intact to prevent escape of water into the premises below

- defined hours within which no sound from within the flat is to be audible outside it

- no bicycles to be left in the common parts

- The demised premises to include glass in external windows so broken glass is paid for by the lessee

- Window frames and the front door and frame of the flat are the responsibility of the lessee

APPENDIX 3: USEFUL WEBSITES AND SOURCES OF INFORMATION

Companies House: for a full list of the FAQs on the Companies House website go to:

www.companieshouse.gov.uk

The Institute of Directors: you can download their four page Factsheet on the duties, responsibilities and liabilities of directors:

www.iod.com/MainWebSite/Resources/Document/dutiesresponsibilities_1006.pdf

The Institute of Chartered Accountants of England and Wales: has some useful resources in their library:

www.ICAEW.com/en/library/subject-gateways/law/company-law/directors-duties

The Leasehold Advisory Service (LEASE): has a range of Advisory Guides on block management issues:

www.lease-advice.org

The Association of Residential Managing Agents (ARMA): you can download Lessee Advisory Notes including LAN 14 on the Companies Act 2006 and LAN 23 on Residents Management Companies:

www.arma.org

APPENDIX 4: **COMPANIES HOUSE FORMS**

	2006 Form	1985 Form
To appoint a Company Director	AP01	288a
To appoint a Corporate Director	AP02	288a
To appoint a Company Secretary	AP03	288a
To appoint a Corporate Secretary	AP04	288a
To resign a Company Director	TM01	288b
To resign a Company Secretary	TM02	288b
Change of Director's details	CH01	288c
Change of Corporate Director's details	CH02	288c
Change of Secretary's details	CH03	288c
Change of Corporate Secretary's details	CH04	288c
To change the registered office	AD01	287
Annual Return	AR01	363